Christine de Buzon

The Château of
CHAMBORD

BONECHI

Facing page: *Bird's-eye view of the south facade surrounded by greenery. On the right, the remains of the stables of Marshal de Saxe.*

Above: *The large north facade and the Cosson running in its channel.*

THE CHATEAU OF CHAMBORD

The château of Chambord is the largest and most imposing of the châteaux of the Loire which were enlarged and renovated between 1450 and 1525. This extraordinary monument to the magnificence of the reign of a builder-king, Francis I, stands in the midst of a park whose walls enclose an immense hunting reserve as large as Paris in area. The simple grandeur of this incomparable site highlights the quality of the daring architecture and the discriminating abundance of sculptured decoration. Italian influence (Domenico da Cortona and, above all, Leonardo da Vinci) has left its mark on the château, while the names of three master masons who worked here are also known (Sourdeau, Trinqueau and Coqueau). It is first and foremost the château of Francis I and the symbol of his power and prestige.

THE TWO PRINCIPAL FACADES

The four towers of the long **northeast facade** (photo above), survivors of the medieval manor architecture, vertically articulate the imposing facade. On the east (to the left in the photo) is the tower with the apartments of Francis I; on the west, the chapel tower with stained-glass windows and surmounted by a cross.

Symbolically this idea of a symmetrical placement of God and the king is exceedingly bold.

All the windows on the first floor between the two central towers of this facade let light into the apartments of Louis XIV. The highest tower of the château, in the background, is called the lantern. It houses a staircase that leads to a small terrace (not open to the public) on which stands a skylight surmounted by an immense crown and a colossal fleur-de-lys. The presence of this emblem of the kings of France at the top of the lantern demonstrates the royal will to underscore its might.

The general plan of the château is visible from the **south facade** or entrance. Beyond the low wall pierced by the Port Royale, an immense square building flanked by four round towers, the donjon or keep, is connected by corridors to the tower with the apartments of the king Francis I on one side, and on the other to the chapel tower. These two towers are in turn connected to the low enclosure wall by two set at right angles, wings. The wall encloses a court of honor on three sides, and the low-storied terraced structures served as dependencies without concealing the view of the apartments in the keep. The presence of unfinished stairs proves that originally this wall was to have been raised.

3

The west facade of the château, from the chapel tower to the Princes' tower, and the porte Dauphine.

THE COLORS OF CHAMBORD

The château is built of micaceous chalk, a soft white stone which lends itself to sculpture but does not resist well to the wear and tear of time. The basement is in Beauce limestone which is more resistant. Most of the construction material for the château was brought in by barge on the Loire as far as the neighboring port of Saint-Dyé. The slate roofs and the geometric decoration on the dormers and chimneys above the level of the terraces recall the use of marble in Italian buildings. They have been repeatedly restored. In the times of Francis I, the roofs were also decorated with gilded lead, much to the marvel of visitors.

Before entering the château, the visitor first of all moves around the wing of the chapel, then along the Dauphine's wing and that of the Princes.

The chapel, two stories high, is housed on the first floor and flanked by the tower as far as the Dauphine's wing. From the outside it is identified by the 19th-century stained-glass windows. The pavilion of the Dauphine's wing consists of four levels, but it is lower than the donjon. It is reached by the Henry II staircase in the Court of Honor and by the staircase in the round turret surmounted by a small dome visible in the photo.

The Princes' wing is situated in the low wall at present covered with terraces. About twelve years ago apartments to be used provisionally by the Presidency of the Republic were installed in the mezzanine. Behind the wall, the imposing mass of the keep is only partially hidden and what the observers note first of all is the striking contrast between the facades and the fine lacework of the sculptured decoration on the upper parts of the château, above the level of the terraces.

Following pages: *Bird's-eye view of the château, south facade. The light, the simplicity of the surroundings, the beauty of the forest all underscore the splendor of this complex château.*

THE SITE OF CHAMBORD

The site was already occupied in ancient times: what was probably a Merovingian mint was replaced by a first castle of the comtes de Blois dating to the 12th century, remains of which were found under the present château. In the 14th century we know that there was a chapel, a common oven and mills on the Cosson as well as a castle.

The château is mirrored in the Cosson river, a small affluent on the left bank of the Loire which was to give its name to the estate and the château, since Chambord comes from the Celtic Cambo ritos, *the "ford at the bend" of the Cosson. Other buildings in the park of Chambord besides farmhouses and pavilions are the chapel of Maurepas and, at the edge of the south wall, seven kilometers from the present château, the vestiges of the castle of Montfraut (torn*

down in 1778) where Francis I sometimes lodged during the building of the château of Chambord. Lastly, the mound of Vienne and an old Montfraut to distinguish it from its homonym can be identified between the present château and Montfraut.

THE STAGES IN THE CONSTRUCTION

The foundations (partially on piles) of the keep initially planned by the king, its central court flanked by four round towers, were begun in September 1519. The rest of the château was designed and built later. Architecture was a passion with the king and he closely followed work in the construction yard, before and after the involuntary interruption in the years which corresponded to his captivity.

The tower and the wing housing the apartments of Francis I were begun in 1540 and the king was doubt-

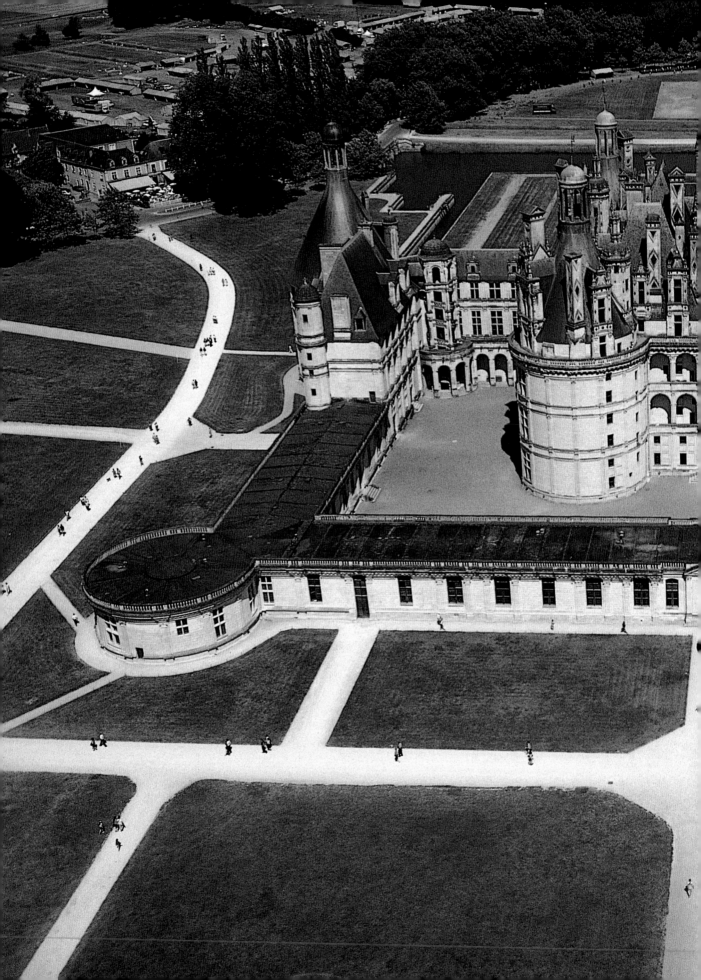

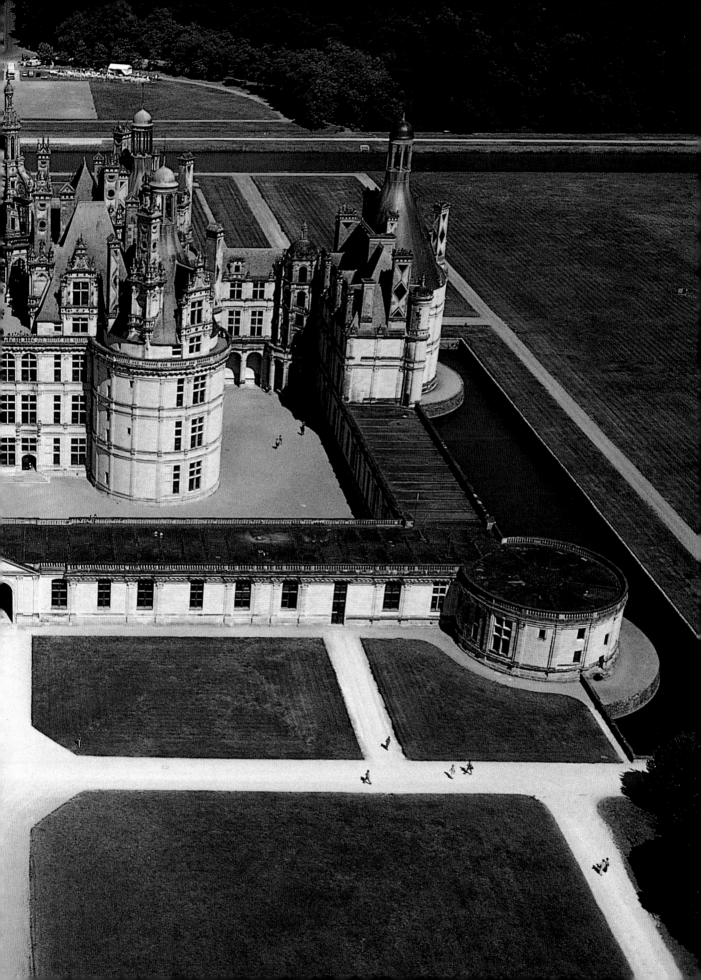

less able to move into them in 1545 and 1546. On his death in 1547, the château had not been finished. While the framework had been done on the chapel wing (it was later reused in Saint-Solenne in Blois), symmetrical with the king's apartments, it had not been covered and bad weather caused serious damage. Work was continued under Henry II but the man responsible for saving the château from ruin was Gaston d'Orléans. It was finally finished by Louis XIV at the end of the 17th century before he began the château of Versailles.

AN ARCHITECTURE OF PRESTIGE

Francis occasionally stayed at Chambord for one or two weeks and received guests of note, in particular Charles V. In 1539, although only the keep was nearing completion it could still serve as a setting for diplomatic maneuvers of the greatest importance.

Above: North facade. The shadows throw the mass of the central towers into relief. The dormers at the top of the towers rival the chimneys in height "built in a way which makes them resemble small châteaux, since they are very large and practically square, very tall and all wrought with black and white stone so that they seem more an embellishment of the château than as something to be used". (Moraes, 1541).

Below: East wing, ground floor. The state carriages of the comte de Chambord.

Charles V was received with all possible splendor. The château had been furnished for the occasion and was decorated with hangings (damasks, taffetas, black and gold velvet decorated with the imperial eagles). According to the king's secretary, Claude Chappuis:

"Perfumes were burnt and flowers and herbs were strewn throughout the superb rooms in honor of the emperor".

Francis's rival marveled at the arrangement of the château and he "considered it a synthesis of what human industry of the time can accomplish".

Evidence of the fame of Chambord in the 1540s, even before its completion, appears in a famous romance, Amadis de Gaule (Book IV, 1544), where the plan and a view of Chambord illustrate the description of an ideal castle. Moreover Francisco de Moraes, writer of romans and secretary of a Portuguese ambassador who seems to have visited Chambord in 1541 and who was greatly impressed by the size of the place, affirmed that the "château has four gates for the four parts of the world". He added that "the most extraordinary invention of this château is a spiral staircase which is at the center of the crossing of the four rooms".

Above: keep, ground floor. The beginning of the double staircase, its pillars with sculptured capitals and the balustrade.

Below: keep, ground floor. One arm of the cross-shaped hall.

THE GREAT DOUBLE STAIRCASE

There can be no doubt but that the marvel of the château is the great staircase with its two spiral stairways which are superposed and wind around the same central shaft. This shaft, entry to which is on the ground floor, is pierced by openings which make it possible for those taking one of the flights to see those on the other without ever meeting them. Henry James, speaking of this "attraction" in his book on his travels in France, remarked that this staircase was an example of truly majestic wit and was what characterized Chambord. Many great figures (and just as many children) have delighted in the game of the impossible meeting in these two superposed flights of stairs where the impression is that the other person is climbing up in the opposite direction.

The staircase is protected by a balustrade, and like an observation post or loggia, overlooks the cross-shaped halls used for fêtes, balls and concerts and where the brilliant life of the court was concentrated.

Above: keep, first floor, the double spiral staircase. The sculptured decoration on the capitals of the external pillars of the staircase.

Below: keep, second floor, the double spiral staircase and the vaulting with sculptured coffers where the crowned F and the salamander, the emblems of Francis I, alternate.

Above: keep, lantern tower. The vault sculptured with the emblems of Francis I rests on pillars decorated with niches and emphasizes the beginning of the simple spiral, pierced by openings, which is situated above the hollow newel of the double spiral staircase.

Right: keep, lantern tower. The profusion of sculptured decoration and the applications of slate herald the prodigious richness of the ornamentation to be seen at the level of the terraces.

The staircase is set on square pillars decorated with bases and capitals. The sculptured triple capitals are an excellent example of early Renaissance French art, with an incredibile variety of motives that range from the plant and animal world to mythology, etc. The depressed vaults of the cross-shaped rooms on the second floor are decorated with coffers carved with the initials of Francis I and the salamander. The double staircase ascends to the terraces and is crowned by another sculptured vault set around still one more spiral, where the cage continues the hollow newel of the double staircase. Above this vault, and another terrace, the eight flying buttresses rise toward the lantern bearing the fleur-de-lys of France.

Above: the great hall of the apartments of the Dauphine Marie-Anne de Baviere, wife of the Dauphin, son of Louis XIV, known as the Grand Dauphin.

Left: Flanders tapestry of the 17th century. The Rape of the Sabine Women, after Jules Romain.

THE APARTMENTS

The keep of the château of Chambord is divided on each level by a room in the form of a cross, which allows for passage and leads to the central staircase. This arrangement delimits the quarters which contain the apartments.

Two distinct traditions are present in the château of Chambord: the French tradition of the fortified royal or seigneurial mansion, furnished with towers which are as much symbols of power (as in the château of Vincennes) as anything else, is accompanied by the influence of Italian palace and villa architecture. With the wars in Italy, Charles VIII had already attempted to bring the Italian splendors to French soil. The modernity of Italy also found its way into

Right: Portrait of the Dauphine.

Below: a small mezzanine room where prints and objects relating to Henri, duc de Bordeau and comte de Chambord, are preserved. On the left wall: portraits of the comte and the comtesse de Chambord; in the background, the showcase in which the volumes containing the names of those who subscribed to Chambord are kept; on the mantel, a white marble bust of Henri, around 1843.

French architecture on the banks of the Loire when the nouveaux riches, powerful and close to the king, had the châteaux of Bury (no longer extant) and Chenonceau built.

Francis I invited Leonardo da Vinci to France and gave him various commissions, notably that of a royal palace in Romorantin that was never built. Leonardo died in the manor of Cloux (Clos-Lucé) near Amboise (this private manor can be visited and contains a collection of models of some of this great artist's inventions) in the spring of 1519, only a few months before construction of Chambord was begun. The influence of Leonardo on the château of Chambord has been studied by J. Guillaume. Leonardo left drawings of superposed flights of stairs for military purposes and for central plan churches with a dome. The principle of a four-armed cross-shaped room is to be found in St. Peter's basilica in Rome, begun by Bramante in 1507 and at Chambord this prin-

Above: keep, ground floor. The room known as «des Soleils» because the wainscotting which comes from the apartment of Gaston d'Orléans, brother of Louis XIII, is decorated with a sun. The fine inner shutters with carved decoration are also still there. Some of this woodwork was donated by the comte de Chambord to one of his followers, O. de Rochebrune, who installed it in the château of Terre-Neuve in Vendée. This room is decorated with portraits of the sovereigns connected with the history of the château (on the left, Charles X and on the right, Stanislas Leszczynski) and a Brussels tapestry of the 15th century, Abraham's Calling, *after Bernard van Orley.*

Below: Painting by Baron Gerard, The Duc d'Anjou Acknowledged King of Spain.

ciple was combined with that of apartments with a regular layout. There are eight on each level: four are housed in the square keep, the other four are placed in the round towers. The principle of a regular ground plan had already been adopted in the Tuscan villas.

Each apartment is composed of a large hall and four smaller rooms on the mezzanine (cabinets and wardrobes). At the juncture of the tower and the keep, two other small mezzanine rooms were to serve as oratory. In the apartments in the keep, the small rooms are set along one of the longer sides of the great hall. In the round towers, they are housed on each of the longer sides.

Fireplaces in the great hall and the superposed cabinets ensured comfort. Communication was by means of small inner stairways and stairs known as "from top to bottom" which really did lead to apartments situated in the terrace pavilions and with the same layout.

Right: *Louis XIII.* Below, left: *Portrait of Charles X.*
Below, right: *Portrait of Louis XV.*

THE CURRENT DECOR OF CHAMBORD

For historical reasons the château was never able to preserve a suitable set of furnishings and few documents are extant (except for inventories) which permit us to reconstruct the various stages of the interior decoration. The State took possession of the property in 1930 and an enormous restoration project was undertaken between 1962 and 1972 on the foundations and in giving the surroundings a semblance of their original aspect. As early as 1840 when the first list was prepared, the château was classified a Historical Monument.

After 1970, efforts turned to the restoration of the interior of the château and important work was done on the lantern tower in 1990-1991. It was decided to furnish the apartments with furniture of outstanding note for none other would be suitable to the majesty of the surroundings. Donations, acquisitions and permanent loans have made it possible to restore life to these immense rooms.

On the ground floor (which can be used for receptions – information to be had at the Caisse nationale des Monuments historiques et des Sites) and on the first floor are those rooms which evoke memories of the king or great personages who stayed at Chambord: apartments of Francis I, of Louis XIV and the queen (recently opened to the public), room of the mementos of the comte de Chambord, etc.

On the second floor are to be found the collections of the Musée de la Chasse et de la Nature which recall the cynegetic vocation of the Estate.

FRANCIS I, CHAMBORD AND THE HUNT

The terrible tale of Thibaud le Tricheur, comte de Blois, tells how as punishment for his crimes he was condemned by God to hunt the same stag in eternity without ever bringing it to bay. It is said that on autumn evenings this ghostly hunt can be heard passing through the sky of Chambord but that no one has ever seen it. As almost all the kings of France, Francis I, and before him Louis XI in the forest of Chinon, was an indefatigable hunter, and it was this love of the chase that led to the creation of the Estate of Chambord. Francis I, an extraordinary enthusiast, enlarged the estate by adding the surrounding lands and in 1542 ordained an enclosing wall to be built (present length: 33 km). On the one hand, the wall was to protect the large animals from poachers, and on the other, the lands bordering the park from the damage these animals might do to the crops. On the side of the forest of Boulogne, the wall remained incomplete until work was resumed by order of Gaston d'Orléans. The year he died, Francis I created a captaincy of the hunt which continued until it was suppressed by Louis XIV.

The landscape was highly varied in 1577 when the Venetian ambassador Jérôme Lippomanno visited Chambord: "the interior of the park in which the castle is situated is filled with forests, lakes, brooks, pastures and hunting sites and in the middle stands a fine building with its gilded battlements, the wings covered with lead, its pavilions, its terraces, its galleries, as our romance writers would describe the abode of Morgan or Alcine [...] We left there stupefied or rather confounded".

Facing page: keep, ground floor, Francis I's hunting room. It is furnished with a series of tapestries dating to the late 16th century, L'histoire des chasses du roi François, *woven to cartoons by Laurent Guyot in the Paris manufacture, the atelier of Faubourg Saint-Germain.*

Below: detail of a tapestry showing Francis I getting ready for a hunt run.

Details of the tapestries with L'historie des chasses du roi François.

Facing page: *the bedchamber of Francis I in the northeast tower. The great Renaissance fireplace and the canopied bed. Francis I's bedchamber was finished a year before his last stay and no longer has any of its original decoration.*

Above: *one of the carved wooden doors, a folding chair and the marquetry chest stand out against the red velvet background.*

THE APARTMENTS OF FRANCIS I

The bedchamber of Francis I

According to documents of the time, the bedchamber of Francis I was in the northeast corner tower of the wall, on the main floor. This is without doubt the coldest room in the castle. The bed and the walls were hung with red velvet, and the fine 16th-century embroidery appliques in gold and silver thread with their plant motives are of Italian origin. The room is furnished soberly with chests, one of which is remarkable for its marquetry work, and folding chairs which recall the fact that the king and his court often moved from one château to another.

This room also contains the copy of a bust of the king that is in the Louvre.

"*Woman is fickle, unhappy he who trusts her*". It was here that Brantôme affirmed he saw this inscription incised by the king himself in the embrasure of a window and not on the window pane, as legend, and an engraving (see illustration following page), would have it.

This room was used as bedroom by Gaston d'Orléans, Louis XII's brother, Philippe d'Orléans, Louis XIV's brother, and then by Catherine Opalinska, queen of Poland. The door carved with a salamander surmounted by a closed crown and sown

with small flames, conceals the staircase "from top to bottom" which leads out of the tower. Like all the others, the apartments of Francis I consist of one large room with four others on the mezzanine. But it is unique in having an extra private study and a very long council room in the adjacent pavilion and which seems to have been meant for use as an audience hall.

The private study of Francis I

Unquestionably this is one of the most remarkable and most admired rooms in the château. It abuts on the tower as attested to by the rounded walls. A staircase below this room, not built until the 20th century, was to allow the king to descend to the terrace at the foot of the château.

The room has a barrel vault, unlike the cross-shaped rooms on the second floor of the keep, and it is lighted by openings set along two of the sides. The roof has been turned into a balustraded terrace and overlooks the great north facade.

Study or oratory? Undoubtedly the difference between the two was negligible in the 16th century. It should be noted howewer that there is nothing religious about the important sculptured decoration. The emblems of Francis I, salamander and initials, found everywhere in the château, are joined by fleurs-de-lys and the arms of France, held by two putti.

This room was called oratory in 1565 and effectively was used as such by the queen under the reign of Louis XIV and then at the time of the queen Catherine Opalinska, as can be seen in an engraving on one of the walls which shows an altar set in front of one of the walled-up arched openings.

Souvent femme varie, Bien fol est qui s'y fie.

Above: *cabinet of Francis I, the only external structure, with carved coffers in the barrel vault and with the door that leads to the gallery.*

Below: *engraving by Desnoyers (19th cent.) after Richard, showing the king together with his sister Marguerite de Navarre.*

GASTON D'ORLÉANS
IN CHAMBORD

Architecture was one of the passions of Gaston d'Orléans. The work he undertook in the château of Blois and which he had entrusted to the architect François Mansart was definitively brought to a halt in 1638. When he decided to reorganize the park of Chambord (1639) and the surroundings of the château, and later renovate the building itself (1640-41) where he loved to stay, before it deteriorated further, he found himself face to face with a considerable task. The restoration was never finished, probably for want of funds, but much work was accomplished in the great cross-shaped rooms and in the lantern tower threatened by the collapse of two of its flying buttresses.

Gaston d'Orléans occupied the bedroom of Francis I and he was probably responsible for dividing the great audience hall which occupied the entire main floor of the east wing into a large square room which received light from both facades, a corridor and two other rooms.

Keep, first floor. One of the four stoves in Meissen majolica (1749) with the arms of Marshal de Saxe, which were once installed in each of the arms of the cross-shaped room on the first floor of the keep. The three other stoves were sold during the Revolution.

Above: *bedchamber of Louis XIV (1643-1715),
furnished in 1681. It was used by Stanislas Leszczynski
(1725-33) and served as gala chamber for Marshal de
Saxe (1748). On this occasion the room was panelled
with woodwork carved by Desgoulons and Roumier in
1723 for the octagonal cabinet of the duchesse
d'Orléans in Versailles. On the mantel in Languedoc
marble, a clock of 1695.*

Left: *bedchamber of the queen Marie-Thérèse of
Austria (1638-1683), later of the marquise de Maintenon
(after 1685) in the apartments of the adjacent tower.
This chamber was refurbished in 1874 by the marquis
de Polignac for a visit by the queen Marie-Antoinette
which never took place.*

THE APARTMENTS OF LOUIS XIV

With Louis XIV, construction works of much greater entity were undertaken and this magnificent abode, declared uninhabitable in the 20th century, was brought back to life. Not only did he reorganize the interior, but he undertook to finish the château, entrusting the work to Jules Hardouin-Mansart (chapel wing and an additional story over the service area), creating an esplanade on the south including the service buildings (not built) and finally reorganizing the surroundings by building immense stables (demolished in 1755) meant to hold 300 horses. The work to be done in the chapel was very important. The tower had never been roofed and the vaulting itself was incomplete.

As for the low wall, mansard roofs were added on the west and on the south, eliminated in the 20th century since they were in poor condition. In 1666 the parish requested by the inhabitants of the town was created and the construction of the church of Saint-Louis was begun three years later.

The two other modifications decided by Louis XIV were the substitution of the entrance gate of the château with the present Porte Royale with its classical pediment and the installation of the royal apartments in the first floor of the keep. Louis XIV modified Francis I's plan by closing one of the arms of the cross-shaped hall (1668). His apartments, a suite "a la française", consisted principally of three large rooms, with parquetry floors, two of them serving as antechambers. Louis XIV's bedroom is preceded by a small room meant for a valet, in which an 18th-century folding bed found in the attic of the château has been set.

The royal bedchamber

The contrast between the apartments of Francis I and those of Louis XIV are striking: parquetry floors, wainscotting, marble fireplaces, mirrors, objects and furniture, all played a part in providing these rooms furnished in the 17th century with a bit of comfort while still maintaining their grandeur and magnificence. The royal bedchamber has recently been decorated in red with gilded wainscotting from

Above: portrait of king Louis XIV.

Below: portrait of François d'Aubigné (1635-1719), marquise de Maintenon. Louis XIV secretly married her after the death of Marie-Thérèse.

Apartments of Louis XIV, first antechamber.

Facing page: *first antechamber. Details of two Sèvres vases ordered by Charles X in 1823-24 and acquired by the State in 1988.*

the château of Versailles. The floor is covered with a carpet from the Savonnerie workshops with the coats of arms of France (18th century). The king usually stayed here about three weeks and one can imagine what the etiquette and the fêtes, similar to those in Versailles, must have been like. Some have gone down in history.

On October 6, 1669, Molière and Lulli presented *Monsieur de Pourceaugnac*, presumably in the south arm of the cross-shaped hall on the first floor that had been transformed into a theater. We learn that the presentation was in danger of being cancelled when Molière fell ill and that Lulli offered to take his place. The king never cracked a smile at the witticisms of the actors. Lulli "ran, danced, frisked about and Louis not even a smile! Finally, hoping to get him to laugh, Lulli went back on stage, and with a running start jumped with both feet into the midst of the orchestra, breaking the harpsichord into smithereens, at the risk of breaking both legs. The instrument flew into a thousand pieces... Lulli disappeared into the abyss, his fall was a triumph..." The following year, on October 14, 1670, Molière presented *Le Bourgeois gentilhomme* and the king deigned to laugh at the second performance.

Louis XIV's two antechambers

The **first antechamber** (the enclosed north arm of the cross-shaped hall) houses a collection of paintings, mostly copies of important pictures regarding the history of France, from the château of Rosny-sur-Seine, and given to Chambord in the 19th century by Marie-Caroline de Berry, mother of the comte de Chambord. The room was decorated by Marshal de Saxe who received Madame de Pompadour here, when she came from the neighboring château of Ménars. The huge console or gaming table covered with a slab of Liassic stone was part of the original furnishing.

The large room next to it, called **second antechamber** (see ill. p. 30), was used as a billiard room by Louis XIV. Recently the State has acquired and restored a splendid billiard table that belonged to Charles X which is to be placed here. On the wall a set of tapestries, the *Story of Ulysses*. In the 18th century this room was decorated with trophies Marshal de Saxe had taken at the Battle of Fontenoy but they disappeared during the Revolution.

Over the mantle is a portrait of Louis XIV as Grand Master of the Order of Saint-Esprit.

CHÂTEAU DE CHAMBORD

CHÂTEAU DE CHAMBORD
côté des appartements de François I.er

Above: keep, first floor, first antechamber or Salle de Compagnie. On the left *is a portrait of the dauphin Louis, father of Louis XVI; on the right a portrait of Louis XIV.* Opposite: room of the Dauphine. Bust of Louis XIV, original plaster by Antoine Coysevox (1640-1720), one of this king's favorite sculptors.

THE GUESTS OF LOUIS XV

In 1725 Louis XV installed his father-in-law, the Polish king Stanislas Leszczynski, in Chambord. For a while it was his permanent residence in spite of the fact that the château was often unhealthy because of the poor maintenance of the surroundings. Finally, on August 25, 1746, Louis XV gave Chambord to Marshal de Saxe, the victor of Fontenoy. Between 1748 and 1750, Chambord regained its old splendor. A theater, where the famous Madame Favart made an appearance, was installed on the second floor in the north arm of the cross-shaped hall.

Keep, first floor, first antechamber or Salle de Compagnie. Above, on the left, the portrait of Stanislas Leszczynski (1677-1766), king of Poland. Driven from the throne of Poland, he lived in Chambord from 1725 to 1733, the estate Louis XV had put at his disposal, then in his duchy of Lunéville and Nancy. Above, on the right, portrait of Marie-Josèphine de Saxe, mother of Louis XVI. Opposite, portrait of Henry IV. The portraits of this popular king were frequently found in the legitimist milieux of the 19th century.

Of the beautiful furniture the château received in this period, one of the majolica stoves and the great console still remain in the first antechamber of Louis XIV. Between the death of Marshal de Saxe and the Revolution of 1789, the château was inhabited by the governors of Chambord (the de Saumery family, then duc and marquis de Polignac until 1790). During the French Revolution the estate was looted and in 1793 the furniture was sold at auction but the château itself escaped destruction.

In 1809 Napoleon raised the estate of Chambord to the principality of Wagram and offered it to Marshal Berthier.

When he died in 1815, Napoleon's endowment was suppressed, and the Marshal's widow, princess Elisabeth de Wagram, was no longer able to take over the costs of maintenance. She was authorized to sell the estate by Louis XVIII. One of the various projects proposed was that of parcelling out the estate into building lots, while it was rumored that the

The second antechamber of Louis XIV's apartments.

Facing page: *Gala bed of the comte de Chambord. Made in Nantes in 1873 for Emile Poinçon, it bears the monograms of Henri and his wife Marie-Thérèse de Modène. It was never used. The fleur-de-lys is found everywhere, including the stitched carpet made by the legitimist ladies of Poutou. In the background, full-length portrait of Charles X.*

Bande Noire, a speculation company, was interested in redeeming one building to use as stone quarry. The comte de Calonne, together with the duchesse de Berry, then opened a subscription in favor of the young Henri, duc de Bordeaux, born on September 29, 1820 and called "the miracle child" because he was born after his father, the duc de Berry, had been assassinated (Feb. 13, 1820), and who seemed to be the sole hope of the legitimists. In 1828 the duchesse de Berry placed the first stone for the restoration of the château. In the meanwhile, after the revolution of July (1830), the king Charles X, the duchesse de Berry and the duc de Bordeaux went into exile.

Henri at the time bore the courtesy title of comte de Chambord in homage to the French who had offered him this symbol of the monarchy. He passed his life far from France and came to Chambord only once to sign the *Manifeste du Drapeau Blanc*, which can be read engraved in marble in this hall on the first floor of the keep where his keepsakes are collected. On his death the estate passed to his Austrian heirs. The French government acquired it in 1917 after legal proceedings. Various objects evoking his memory have been collected in the apartments of Monseigneur le Dauphine, the son of Louis XIV.

Pièce de 4 de campagne

Facing page: *the miniature battery of artillery offered to the comte de Chambord as a child. In the form of play he learned his profession of king and became acquainted with the objects he would one day have to use.*

Above: *painting by Dubuffe depicting the birth of the duc de Bordeaux in the palace of the Tuileries. Marie-Caroline de Berry presents her son Henri to the guard in the presence of the king Louis XVIII. The young elder sister of the future pretendent to the throne of France, Louise de France, is shown on the left of the picture.*

Right: *detail of the gala bed of the comte de Chambord.*

MEMENTOS OF THE COMTE DE CHAMBORD

Various objects go back to his youth. The plaster statue shows him as captain of the Lancers, under the portrait of his mother Marie-Caroline de Berry, made as a pendant to the statue of Henry IV as a child and with reference to the fact that the duc de Bordeaux could have reigned under the name of Henry V. The miniature artillery battery with cannons that actually worked was given to him by the commanding officer Ambroise.

Other mementos which refer to various moments of his life outside France include the picture of Charles-X's last moments in exile, the equestrian portrait of the comte de Chambord by Schwiter, a view of the Grand Canal in Venice, a bust signed by

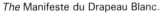
The Manifeste du Drapeau Blanc.

Equestrian portrait of the comte de Chambord by Baron de Schwiter. In the background on the left the silhouette of Venice can be distinguished.

Charron. In the adjacent rooms are the bust of Henry V and the model in bronze on a wood pedestal of the equestrian statue of the comte de Chambord by Gérard.

The collections of the château of Chambord also include the throne of Henry V (not on exhibition), the volumes of the national subscription for Chambord, and a series of propaganda objects which were given out after 1830: small boxes with the picture of Henry or Louise, a great number of engravings showing Marie-Caroline during her captivity in Blaye or her children, medals given on various occasions.

The *Manifeste du Drapeau Blanc* or *Manifeste de Chambord* is dated Chambord, July 5, 1871. The Assembly had just abrogated the law relating to the exile of the princes of the house of Bourbon and the comte de Chambord decided to visit France incognito. The *Manifeste* announced a program: "administrative decentralization and local franchises", public freedoms, an "honorably practiced" universal suffrage and control of the two Chambers. The white ensign (royal standard of France) was also evoked. "I

will no longer let the standard of Henry IV, Frances I and Joan of Arc be wrested from my hands... I received it as a holy pledge from the old king, my ancestor who died in exile; it is still inseparable for me as a keepsake of my distant fatherland; it flew over my cradle, I want it to cast a shadow on my tomb."

During the exile of the legitimist pretendant and particularly during the long period in which he lived in the castle of Frohsdorf (Austria), the Estate of Chambord was administered by loyal followers including Joachim Barrande "general representative" who forwarded the requests for aid that came from all of France to Austria. He was also in charge of the restoration that began in 1850 and which continued despite the death of the count (1883) and of the comtesse de Chambord (1886). The duc de Parme and the comte de Bardi continued to set aside the income from the estate for the restoration of the château which had in the meanwhile become urgent. The château had served as a hospital in 1871 and the woodwork had been used as firewood to keep the wounded soldiers warm. The architects Desbois, father and son, were entrusted with the work. In 1890 they restored and even reconstructed the lantern and the skylight (see the originals in the small lapidary museum). The sole heir, R. de Parme, died in 1907.

His firstborn son, prince Elie, had made a career for himself in the Austrian army and, in 1914, the Estate of Chambord was sequestered. The French government came into possession in 1930 at the end of a lawsuit. Restoration work directed by Maurice Lotte and then by Grenouillot was accellerated with the approach of World War II when the château received a part of the collections of the Louvre. After 1945, up until 1974, the work was entrusted to Michel Ranjard.

There were two principal aims adopted in renovating the interior of Chambord: that of evoking the great figures connected with its history and that of giving life to the immense spaces of the building, monument of French royalty. The keep had been

Opposite: portrait of Charles X in coronation dress.

Below: Charles X receiving extreme unction (November 6, 1836) from the hands of Cardinal de Latil who had consecrated him king at Reims. At the foot of the bed, his grandchildren, Henri and Louise.

Keep, first floor, the room known as "the Oleander
Room", installed in 1784 in the old dining room of
Marshal de Saxe. In the center, the Polish style bed
(second half of the 18th century). In order to reduce the
volume of the room, the ceiling was lowered. This room
contains a view of Chambord by Van der Meulen, a
portrait of Racine by Largillière, on the wall between the
window and the fireplace, and the portraits of the
comtes d'Artois and de Provence.

36

conceived as a gala setting, the symbolic place where the court and the monarch met, the ideal site for diplomatic encounters between the monarch and his rivals. The present decoration of the château on the first floor perpetuates this vision of royal Chambord, symbol of the prestige of political power. While the château was not often lived in, it was used by important guests and their portraits serve to underscore and help this imposing building live once more.

After the Revolution, whose aim had been to do away with the monarchs or at least destroy the emblems of royalty (it is said that Chambord was saved because the architect exaggerated the estimates of demolishing it), projects multiplied. Throughout the centuries there have been dozens of ideas of what to do with this utopian palace, some grandiose and others less so. As early as 1529, according to the Comptes des Menus Plaisirs of the king, Francis I had asked Pietro Caccia, hydraulic engineer, how to go about deviating a part of the course of the Loire up to Chambord so it could bathe the base of his château. Under Napoleon it was to have become the

Opposite: *Portrait of Louis XV.*

Below: *detail of the fabric of the hangings, copy of an 18th-century painted silk.*

seat of an educational establishment for the Legion of Honor (a decree of 1806 never applied).

It was also considered turning it into an agricultural settlement. Paul-Louis Courier and, later, Eugène Sue (1848) developed the idea of a phalanstery Chambord with a model factory, agricultural school, "hospital", hospice, schools etc. Chambord was to have become a "terrestrial paradise" (Eugène Sue).

The utopian dreams of the "phalansterists" (Fourierist cooperative community) tended to center on Chambord, for the imposing château is magnificently isolated and its proportions seem superhuman.

Everything in Chambord has to be exceptional. Even now the town, the town hall and the burying-grounds are all let out to the State.

Above, the keep, 2nd storey,
one arm of the cross-shaped hall.
These vaulted rooms have tiled
floors and are heated.

Below: detail of a coffered carved vault.

Facing page: the west wing, the
chapel tower, the exterior staircase of
Henry II and the corridor which leads
to the keep, seen from the terraces.
The staircase turret, illuminated by
large openings, is surrounded
outside, at the height of the first floor,
by an external gallery set on arcades,
which doubles the internal gallery on
two levels. The sculptured decor of
the Henry II staircase was never
completed. The summit apparently
was to have had herms, the column
statues which decorate the external
Francis I staircase, its symmetrical
pendant in the east court of honor.
Here the stone has only been roughly
hewn. The last level of the staircase,
the dormers and the covering of the
wing and the chapel tower were not
completed until 1685. The stylistic
difference in the treatment of the
dormer windows is evident: in the
gallery, the dormer is highly
decorated and is a kind of model of
early Renaissance decorative
elements; on the west wing the
dormers have classic pediments.

Above: keep, second floor, Salle de Diane. The series of tapestries woven in the Manufacture of Paris, atelier of Faubourg Saint-Marcel, depict the Story of Diana after cartoons by Toussaint Dubreuil.

Left, statue in white marble, Diane Calysto (1892) by Alexandre Falguière (1831-1900). A showcase includes bronze statuettes, among them a Diana by Houdon.

Facing page: Keep, second floor, Marion Schuster Trophy Room.
Following page: The woodwork panels come from the château of Bercy. A crossbow and some knives are displayed in the showcase.

THE HUNTING MUSEUM

On the second floor, the collections of the Hunting Museum (Le Musee de la Chasse et de la Nature: Fondation Jacqueline et François Sommer, created in 1966) constitute an annex to the Paris museum of Hôtel Guénégaud. The Foundation represents a center of influence as regards hunting with dogs and encourages and assists hunters and those who defend nature.

The collections dealing with the hunt, and with arms (16th-19th centuries) and a collection of trophies (gift of Marion Schuster) keep company with a set of fine tapestries.

In the smaller rooms, other objects having to do with the chase are assembled: glass, faïence, sculpture, hunting knives, warders' badges, dress buttons, etc.

Pieces of furniture, occasionally of particular interest, house various objects of art, paintings, engravings and lithographs. A great number of trophies and a few stuffed animals complete this historical evocation of the world of the hunt. Chambord, rendezvous for hunters, royal monument, marvelous example of early Renaissance French architecture, European wildlife reserve, is also a place of inspiration for writers who surrender to the magic of this place.

For François-René de Chateaubriand, for example, in his *Vie de Rancé*, the silhouette of Francis I's palace was seen as an arabesque or became the image of a woman's tresses flying skywards.

"From far off, the building is an arabesque; it looks

Above: *keep, second floor, François Sommer Hall. A series of tapestries woven in the Gobelins Manufacture after cartoons by Le Brun (second half of the 17th century), depicts the* Story of Meleager: Hunting the Calydonian Boar, The Encounter with Castor and Pollux, Meleager Presenting the Boar's Head to Atalante, Althea, Meleager's Mother, Throwing the Fatal Log into the Fire. Opposite: *keep, second floor, Flemish Hall. Tournai tapestry, around 1530, depicting a* Wolf Hunt.

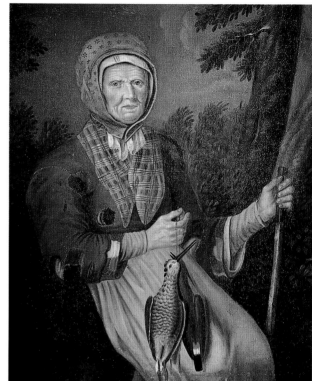

Keep, second floor, Flemish Hall: two portraits.

like a woman whose tresses the wind has blown into the air; from close up this woman becomes part of the masonry and changes into towers; then it is Clorinde reclining on the ruins. The caprice of the sculptor's touch is ever present and the delicacy and lightness of feature appears again in the image of a dying woman warrior. When you move closer still the fleur-de-lys and the salamander materialize on the ceilings. If Chambord were ever to be destroyed, one would not find the early Renaissance style anywhere, for in Venice it is a medley."

To cite just one more example, Alfred de Vigny, in a famous passage in *Cing-Mars*, a historical novel that appeared in 1826, describes the château as follows: "One would say that, imprisoned in some marvelous lamp, a geni of the east had carried it off from the land of the sun during one of the thousand nights to conceal it in the land of mists, with the loves of a handsome prince. This palace is kept secret like a treasure, and with its blue domes, its elegant minarets, standing round on great walls or soaring into the air, its long terraces which overlook the woods, its light spires which oscillate in the wind, its interlaced crescents everywhere on the colonnades, one would think oneself in the realms of Bagdad or Kashmir were it not for the blackened walls, the carpets of moss and ivy, and the pale and melancholy color of the sky which proclaim it to be a land of rain". The château of four hundred and forty rooms which Francis I never lived to see achieved is now set under the safekeeping of its seven hundred thousand annual visitors, still fascinated by the finely balanced harmony of its masses, the prestige of its interior spaces and the wealth of its surroundings, and attracted by the spectacles (including a "son et lumière"), concerts, temporary events or fêtes which make Chambord a beacon of international standing".

The keep seen from the low wall and the exuberant ornamentation of the upper parts: pedimented dormer windows, monumental chimneys, shell niches, stair turrets.

Facing page: the terraces of the keep. The pavilions contain apartments and resemble a suspended, marvelously decorated miniature village. The terraces of the château offer a view of the deer runs in all directions. One of the pavilions houses the excellent permanent exhibition "Comprendre Chambord" which completes the visit with documents and models.

THE ESTATE OF CHAMBORD

One of the first vocations of the estate of Chambord is hunting. If the forest is the source of wealth, the hunt is the font of renewed pleasure. Through six gates the estate opens onto the forest of Boulogne on the south and the countryside of Sologne to the north. Its moors, forests and prairies were formerly exploited by farms scattered in the deforested clearings, but in the 19th century (2000 hectares) and in the 20th century (1000 hectares) reforesting was carried out, with a prevalence of evergreen forests over oak. Currently 4800 out of a total of 5343 hectares are covered with woods and ponds.Hunting in Chambord is what gives life to the estate and hunting with dogs is nowadays administered by the presidency of the Republic and the estate and the château still play host, during the hunting season, to illustrious guests, chiefs of state and ministers, both French and foreign.

In 1970 a reserve was created where European wildlife can be studied: deer, wild boars, roe-deer, etc. The deer population is regulated by selective hunting and the capture of animals which are then sent to repopulate other forests. The boars are hunted.

Part of the park (about 1500 hectares) is open to the public, with observatories and three distinct paths marked deer path, roe-deer path, boar path, as well as a general circuit path.

INDEX

ISBN 88-7009-966-0